The Enduring River

*Edgar Lee Masters' Uncollected
Spoon River Poems*

Selected and with an Introduction by
Herbert K. Russell

Southern Illinois University Press • Carbondale and Edwardsville

94   93   92   91   4   3   2   1

Library of Congress Cataloging-in-Publication Data

Masters, Edgar Lee, 1868–1950.
    The enduring river : Edgar Lee Masters' uncollected Spoon River
poems / selected and with an introduction by Herbert K. Russell.
        p.   cm.
    Includes bibliographical references.
    ISBN 0-8093-1685-4 (cloth)
    I. Russell, Herbert K., 1943–   . II. Title.
PS3525.A83A17   1991
811'.52—dc20   90-9922
                                                                    CIP

*Rendering by Roscoe Misselhorn from a rare photograph of the
covered bridge across Spoon River at Duncans Mills. Edgar Lee
Masters made his first crossing of the Spoon River on this bridge on the
morning of July 3, 1880.*

Gone is the court house, in the long ago
By Newton Walker built; gone houses, churches,
Gone streets, however the looker searches;
Gone Proctor's Grove, gone Spudaway below
The village hills, gone with the populace
That walked about, and vanished like a vapor.
For at last a story printed on fragile paper
Outlasts all bronze, all stone that chisels chase.

— "Havana and Lewistown"

Contents

Acknowledgments

Grateful acknowledgment is extended to Hilary Masters, on behalf of Ellen C. Masters, for permission to reprint the poems of Edgar Lee Masters included in this volume.

Introduction

In 1915, the Illinois lawyer Edgar Lee Masters published a book of poems about people who had lived in his boyhood towns of Petersburg and Lewistown and overnight found himself famous with a free-verse bestseller, the *Spoon River Anthology*. The book became "the most read and most talked-of volume of poetry that had ever been written in America" (as one critic phrased it), and is today recognized as a twentieth-century landmark of literature.

Spoon River was the first part of a literary triad marking what Carl Van Doren once called "the revolt from the village"—an abandonment of nineteenth-century genteel expressions for harsher portrayals of American life. Sherwood Anderson would add a second part of the triad in 1919 with *Winesburg, Ohio*, a collection of interrelated short stories that he began after reading *Spoon River*. Sinclair Lewis would add the third part in 1920 with his novel of village life, *Main Street* (and subsequently acknowledge America's literary indebtedness to Masters in his 1930 Nobel Prize acceptance speech).

Such was the reception given these works that all three writers returned to the small-town scenes of their literary triumphs: Masters in an imitative sequel to his anthology, *The New Spoon River* (1924); Anderson with such stories as "Death in the Woods" and "The Egg"; and Lewis in well-known novels such as *Elmer Gantry* and *Babbitt*.

Less well known, even among scholars, is that Masters wrote dozens of other poems set in the area he made famous as "Spoon River." A chief reason for the obscurity of these writings is that he scattered them through more than two dozen volumes of miscellaneous verses and verse dramas, making them virtually impossible for the average reader to find. Because Masters never called attention to these poems as a potential third collection of Spoon River writings, many of them have remained out of sight and out of mind for three-quarters of a century.

In reviewing the books in which these were published, it seemed to me for a variety of reasons that they ought to receive new attention in a self-contained volume. In endeavoring to fashion such a volume, I have selected only poems deriving from three west-central Illinois counties: Menard County, where Masters spent his first Illinois years in and around Petersburg; Fulton County, where he spent his adolescence and young manhood in Lewistown; and Mason County, a narrow connecting link to the first two.

I have confined myself to this area for two reasons: it is the source of many of the poems that make up the book for which Masters is chiefly known, *Spoon River Anthology;* and the poems selected—lyrical, tender, and nostalgic—form an interesting and useful counterpoint to the brooding diatribes, ironies, and denunciations that make up much of *Spoon River.* To put it another way, the poems in this book show an elegiac side of Masters that will be unfamiliar to many readers. But this side needs also to be presented in order to illustrate his intellectual diversity and artistic complexity.

Likewise, the form of many of these poems stands in contrast to the free-verse lines of *Spoon River Anthology.* These herein tend to be conventional in versification, with traditional stanza arrangements, regular meter, and frequent rhymes. They come from ten different volumes, including his first (*A Book of Verses,* 1898) and his last (*Along the Illinois,* 1942), and include five pieces from a posthumous volume (*The Harmony of Deeper Music,* 1976) compiled from the twelve thousand items of Mastersiana at the University of Texas at Austin. Collectively, these poems written across a span of more than half a century also show Masters' poetic range in a second way—that of style.

Unfortunately, Masters was also capable of publishing much inferior verse or cluttering his writing with his own parochial opinions. Because of this, I have omitted entirely poems representing poor writing performances by Masters. I have, however, included certain polemical discussions where I felt the poetry justified it. The result, I think, yields a harmonious balance, especially in the areas of politics and religion, subjects which often teased Masters' attention away from the poetry at hand and into personal propaganda. It was, for example, a belief of his that the Civil War could have been avoided, that it was a permanent blight on the American dream as conceived by the country's founders. This idea is repeated in this volume in the poem "Memorabilia," in which a member of the Rutledge family illustrates this belief. But Masters could also discern humorous instances deriving from this conflict, as he did in another poem, "Achilles Deatheridge," in which a Menard County private accidentally arrests General Grant. Likewise, one finds some of Masters' favorite dislikes about religion repeated in the poem "Concord Church," in which the strict religiousness of Calvinism is taken to task. But this is offset by a more lighthearted view of religion in "The Mourner's Bench," in which the speaker has to decide whether to "get religion" or go to a dance and regain her lost boyfriend.

Most of the selections, however, are more like the opening and closing poems, artistically well done or useful biographically. The former provides the title for this book and also reflects Masters' lifelong fascination with the rural areas of his boyhood:

> Youth is the river towns they knew
> By the enduring river.

The latter provides the book's mood-setting epigraph and theme of *ubi sunt* (where are they now, the people and places of yesteryear?), and also highlights Masters' seriousness about writing as art:

> For at last a story printed on fragile paper
> Outlasts all bronze, all stone that chisels chase.

This, then, is the plan of this volume, presented three-quarters of a century after the publication of *Spoon River Anthology:* to bring together in one place for the first time the best of Edgar Lee Masters' lesser-known poems from the Spoon River area.

The literary village of Spoon River is a composite of two Illinois corn belt county seats: Petersburg, in the heart of the Lincoln country near New Salem and Springfield; and Lewistown, forty miles to the northwest, near the Spoon River. Masters lived in Petersburg (where his father was a lawyer) from age one (in 1869) to eleven, spending a significant portion of the summers at his paternal grandparents' farm five and one-half miles north of town. He adopted a special fondness for these grandparents (Squire Davis and Lucinda Masters) and used them as models for *Spoon River Anthology*'s "Lucinda Matlock" and "Davis Matlock."

Masters also developed a deep affection for the countryside through which he passed on his way to and from their Sand Ridge Township farm.* Because several of these rural places are mentioned in this volume (and in *Spoon River Anthology* and in some of his other books as well), it will be useful to note the landmarks young "Lee" Masters passed on an average day in the late 1870s as he made his way to his grandparents.

To get to the farm, he went northward out of Petersburg up a hill, by the Menard County Fairgrounds, and on for two miles, after which he came to a "country mile" known as Bowman's Lane. Then he had a choice of routes. He could angle northwest toward New Hope Church and the village of Oakford. Or he could take a longer way, northeasterly down Shipley's Hill, the road following the base of the hill with the trees overhanging on one side and the Sangamon River bottoms opening out on the other. He would pass through the bottoms and angle northwest and upwards (on a winding road now abandoned) before reaching the uplands and a view of the Mason County hills to the north. He would proceed westward by Shipley Schoolhouse on its tall hill (the Shipleys were large landowners), and then his grandparents' place would come into view.

The farmhouse stood on a hill, and although situated on the prairie, it was surrounded in every direction by streams: to the south and passing through the farm (and neighbor Sevigne Houghton's woods) was Concord Creek, by which Masters played as a boy; a mile to the west, the headwaters of the Latimore grew significant enough for that stream to have a name; and the Sangamon River flowed three miles to the east, then turned and passed north of the farm as well. (The farmstead is discussed in this volume in the selection entitled "The Old Farm.")

---

*Masters' spelling, punctuation, and capitalization sometimes differed from contemporary norms. Examples in this text include Sandridge (for Sand Ridge), Lattimore (for Latimore Creek), Duncan's Mills (for Duncans Mills), Mason County Hills (versus hills), and Anne Rutledge (versus Ann).

But the people Masters saw on the Petersburg square and those he heard of there were also to be important to him. Petersburg in the 1870s and 1880s was a town of three thousand in a valley framed by hills. The Sangamon River, the Menard County Courthouse, and most of the people were in the valley or on the slopes. The hilltops held the homes of the wealthy along with two cemeteries, Rose Hill, where some of the human models for *Spoon River* are buried, and Oakland, where many of the other *Spoon River* names are found, along with the graves of Ann Rutledge and several pioneers associated with Abraham Lincoln.

Lincoln was very familiar with Petersburg (he had, in fact, surveyed the town when he lived two miles south at New Salem during the years 1831–37). Until he was elected to the presidency, he was a familiar sight in Petersburg, and as a lawyer visited Masters' grandparents' farm north of town, as Masters reported in the 1926 edition (volume 18) of the *Journal of the Illinois State Historical Society:* "Lincoln tried a case before my grandfather under the maple trees in front of the Masters' homestead, for my grandfather was a Justice of the Peace for a time." Lincoln also lost a legal case of his grandfather's. (The paths of the two men still cross, so to speak, a mile west of the farm on the Illinois prairie where Masters Road meets Lincoln Trail.)

The future president left behind scores of acquaintances, many of whom Masters grew up hearing about, such as Bowling Green, the New Salem justice of the peace before whom young Lincoln practiced law, and Jack Kelso, the unambitious New Salem intellectual who shared his knowledge of fishing and books with Lincoln.

In the days when New Salem was a home to such pioneers, it had been a collection of two dozen buildings on a hilltop of three or four acres overlooking the Sangamon River. But by the time Masters came along, Petersburg had long since supplanted New Salem as the trading center of the region, and most of New Salem's buildings had tumbled to decay. An exception was the gristmill, which had been rebuilt on the banks of the Sangamon in 1853. Masters and his boyhood chums played among the ruins of the vanished village or took the bridle path down to the mill and river.

Masters also knew personally many individuals associated with the president, including William Herndon, Lincoln's law partner and eventual biographer and also a law associate, beginning in 1872, of Masters' lawyer-father. (Herndon was an occasional partner in recreational pursuits of the Masters family and was present on the fishing trip to the Sangamon on the day Masters nearly drowned; one such outing minus the near-disaster is described in this volume in "The Old Salem Mill: Petersburg.") Masters also saw on the Petersburg square Mentor Graham (the schoolmaster who straightened out Lincoln's grammar and taught him surveying). Masters was an acquaintance, too, of the Armstrong clan (leaders of the roistering Clary's Grove Boys of New Salem fame), at least three of whom were significant to Lincoln's story. (Masters and the novelist Theodore Dreiser once spent a central Illinois evening listening to one of the Armstrong sons play the fiddle.) Masters also knew John McNamar (the man who jilted Ann Rutledge before her story became entwined with Lincoln's).

Some have suggested that Masters knew too much about Lincoln, for he eventually (in 1931) published the first unfriendly biography of the ex-president and created a storm of controversy wherever the book was read. In fact, *Lincoln: The Man* was so severe with its subject that a bill was introduced in Congress to bar the volume from the mails. Its publication hurt Masters professionally, but it was similar in a way to a good many other things he wrote, including *Spoon River Anthology:* he was usually frank in his writings and seldom pulled punches out of a fear that somebody somewhere might be offended.

The passage of time has done much to ameliorate the harsh first reactions to *Lincoln: The Man,* but even Masters' severest critics might have forgiven him for the eloquence of his statement about another famous New Salem resident, Ann Rutledge. Sixteen years before the Lincoln book, Masters had written so movingly of Lincoln's supposed sweetheart in *Spoon River Anthology* that local historians had turned to it for an epitaph when they placed a new stone over her Petersburg grave in 1921:

Out of me unworthy and unknown
The vibrations of deathless music;
"With malice toward none, with charity for all."
Out of me the forgiveness of millions toward millions,
And the beneficent face of a nation
Shining with justice and truth.

I am Anne Rutledge who sleep beneath these weeds,
Beloved in life of Abraham Lincoln,
Wedded to him, not through union,
But through separation.
Bloom forever, O Republic,
From the dust of my bosom!

In addition to growing up in the shadow of the nineteenth century's preeminent political figure, Masters also heard much of the leading religious figure of the Midwest, Peter Cartwright. The most famous backwoods minister in America, Cartwright was a close acquaintance of Masters' devout grandfather and frequently visited the farm, as Masters noted in his 1942 book, *The Sangamon:* "Cartwright made my grandfather's house a sort of station in his travels to the Spoon River country. He often took Sunday dinner there, and my grandmother had many anecdotes to tell about his quick temper, his racy stories and conversation." (Cartwright is buried at the nearby village of Pleasant Plains.)

These individuals and others, several of them vital to American history, literature, and folk studies, and others important to state history, all came to Masters' attention during his boyhood in Petersburg. Not surprisingly, they eventually showed up in his writings.

In the summer of 1880, Masters' association with the Petersburg–New Salem area changed dramatically when his father decided to move his law practice and family forty miles to the northwest to the county seat of Lewistown in Fulton County. The family loaded its goods on one train and themselves on another and proceeded to the town of Havana where they stayed the night before crossing the Illinois River and continuing by stage on the morning of July 3. Along the way, Masters made his first, if unprepossessing, crossing of the Spoon River:

It was July and very hot. The black flies bit the stage horses, and smells of dank weeds, dead fish, and the green scum of drying pools smote our nostrils. At Duncan's Mills, a place of one store and a post office, we crossed Spoon River on a covered wooden bridge, and ascending a long hill a mile beyond reached the uplands that surround Lewistown.

Lewistown was to be Masters' home for the next eleven years. Like Petersburg, it was also steeped in history (it had once been the county seat for much of northern Illinois, including Chicago), and more importantly for Masters, it afforded him a better education than he could then have had in Petersburg. Lewistown had a high school with a graduate of Princeton serving as principal, and in the 1880s a generally higher level of culture than did the other town. The Lewistown area also had several village intellectuals who had a favorable effect on Masters, including poet Margaret George (whose death is discussed in "The Hills of Big Creek") and Dr. William Strode, a natural scientist whose research in and around the nearby village of Bernadotte (on the Spoon River) attracted national and some international attention. Here Masters would also continue his informal education into the past, learning of such local personages as Newton Walker, who appears in *Spoon River Anthology* as "Major Walker who had talked/With venerable men of the revolution," and who had entertained Lincoln as well (when he visited Lewistown in 1858 to rebut Stephen Douglas' speech at nearby Proctor's Grove).

It was well that Masters received these early educational benefits, for he was to have only one year of higher education (at nearby Knox College in Galesburg). At his father's urging, he studied for the law and passed the Illinois bar exam in 1891. Following a brief partnership with his lawyer-father, Masters moved in 1892 to Chicago, his home for the next thirty years.

He would eventually prosper in Chicago (replacing former Illinois Governor Altgeld in Clarence Darrow's law firm), and meet such literary notables as Theodore Dreiser, who helped find a book publisher for *Spoon River Anthology,* and *Poetry* magazine's Harriet Monroe, who proofed the book's galleys.

Unfortunately, after *Spoon River's* success in 1915, Masters could never duplicate his literary achievement, although he published an additional forty books of poetry, fiction, history, biography, verse dramas, and autobiography as well as short stories and essays.

It was also his misfortune to suffer from an unhappy marriage (begun in 1898 and ended in 1923), and when this finally failed, he left Chicago for New York, his home for much of the rest of his life. A second marriage was more felicitous.

Masters only seldom returned to the towns of his boyhood

after the publication of *Spoon River Anthology*, for there was some enmity against him because of his book, and times and things had changed, and many of the people he had admired were dead or dead to him. But he returned all the time in his mind's eye and in his many books—a point which he was at pains to make in the final sentence of the final "chapter" of his 1936 autobiography, *Across Spoon River:* "Here I am in a [New York] hotel room. All I have to do is to close my eyes and I can look at the Mason County Hills and see my kite among the clouds."

Mason County and to a much larger extent the counties of Menard and Fulton form the geographic emphasis of this volume. Following an opening poem, Masters tells in the second of his strong emotional ties to Petersburg, after which follow several poems about the Spoon River area's most famous citizen, Lincoln, and those who were fundamental to his character and shaping or were themselves shaped by the Civil War. The remaining poems are arranged by place—from Petersburg to Lewistown—the same journey Masters made on July 2–3, 1880. Most of the poems (the first twenty-six) focus on the area around Petersburg, his "heart's home" as he called it, to which he returned, not to leave again, on March 8, 1950.

Masters is buried in Oakland Cemetery on "the hill" in Petersburg next to his beloved grandmother. (She is discussed in this volume in the poem "I Shall Never See You Again.") The grave of Ann Rutledge is forty paces away, and an equal distance beyond are those of Masters' parents, brothers, and sister, and a little farther still that of a favorite boyhood chum. Around all of them are the pioneer dead—famous, infamous, obscure—many of whose stories are crystallized in the pages of *Spoon River Anthology*, and in those which follow.

The Enduring River

River Towns

Far from New York by the ship-traveled sea
Stand the river-towns I knew
Changeless as memory.
They are as the land, they grew
Out of the land as blossoms which matured,
And bloomed no more.
As the land they have endured,
Enclosed by slumbering hills,
At peace by the wharfless shore.

What are great wars to them,
Or the state devoured
By business men, or by new laws restored?
They speak but quiet words around the square.
To them the stratagem
Of cities, banks for toil deflowered,
Of the broken, or the victorious sword,
Are as the river's ripples, the evening air.
They see the fields re-grow, the seasons glide;
Close to the earth they share
Eternal life with nature. The river's tide
Is like their life. Oak groves,
Low lands of elm and sycamore
Are like their hopes, their loves,
Their looking after and before.

Over the sands at Miller's Ford,
Where my uncle fished with me,
The river flows unheedingly
By the swallow-haunted bank.

And Petersburg and Bernadotte,
Havana, a sleeping turtle on the sand,
Preserve their drowsy lot.
Bells toll at times for a notable,
A child, a soldier who sank
In battle afar, brought here at last
To the waiting land.
And for the rest men buy and sell
About the square, recalling names and dates,
And faces of the long ago
Who stood or walked here happy or harassed,
And watched the river's flow,
Which streams today and meditates
Upon the sleeping town, the meaningless past.

Grand Haven by the Lake,
By the river of endless flags,
And level pastures, where the gulls forsake
The roaring water to hover over the dunes,
Dreams on by the timeless quags.
But here the sea seems near,
For the Lake resembles the sea.
But as at Petersburg the town communes
With the earth, and by the earth is quieted here
And voices on the streets are like the sound
Of fainting wind in autumn hollows:
The town is memory longing for the places
Far up the river, never found
By the river's winding spaces
Which the heart forever follows.

Those who have reached the sea return
To Bernadotte no more,
Or Petersburg. They yearn
For Miller's Ford in vain,
For Havana and Grand Haven too.
The sea is as the years which chain
Their steps as Time which never
Frees them to live their youth again.
Youth is the river towns they knew
By the enduring river.

Petersburg

Petersburg is my heart's home. There
I knew at first earth's sun and air;
Still I can see the hills around it,
The people that walked its business square.

Still I can smell the coal mine's smoke
Beside the railroad, see the oak
Upon that hill of Horace Wood's,
One of the best of gentle folk.

And flowed forever the Sangamon
East of the limits, and on and on;
And over the river there was the covered
Bridge near the brewery long since gone.

On Saturdays how thickly walked
Crowds of the pioneers and talked;
They traded at the Broad-gauge store,
Or idly stood, or idly stalked.

Petersburg is built upon some hills
That hem the square of stores and mills,
Lumber yards, wagon shops and churches,
And business buildings and domiciles.

Over the river and to the east
The prairie brings the harvest feast;
And up the hills to the setting sun
The meadows by the winds are breezed.

Crows to the heights forever fly
Over this town in a magic sky;
The air is like an enchantress's crystal,
That seems to hold and to magnify.

So is it too like cellophane
Along that mile called Bowman's Lane,
Beside the Fair Grounds where the field larks
Sing forever the same refrain.

Nestled near where the river creeps
Petersburg like an old man sleeps;
The pioneers are gone, but others
Walk the square where memory keeps.

Thought of the farmers, the Saturdays
When Benjamin Short and Tilford Hays
Stood by the stores and talked of cattle,
Corn and clover and country ways.

Less than two miles by the Springfield road
Is the hill New Salem where flows and flowed
The river by the little first grist-mill
In the days when Jackson's glory glowed.

Rose Hill is over the river and
South of the houses there is Oakland;
Many a bright eye there is hidden
That once this square by the river scanned.

And why they came and why they went,
Why we were into their places sent
Brings wonder that daily overcomes us
For what we mean and what they meant.

The Old Salem Mill: Petersburg

How often in my boyhood I cast my line
Beneath the shadow of Old Salem Mill.
It seemed a towering structure beside the Hill,
Whose roof was mirrored in the saturnine
Water above the dam, whose roof was high
As the trees above the Hill. And there it stood
Lonely and phantom-like against the sky,
With windows which looked on the solitude
Of the hilly east, the turbid river's course.
How often then I climbed the winding road
Between oak trees to look upon the scene
Where the vanished villagers long before abode,
By then a pasture where a cow, a horse
Cropped grass, where business, jollity had been.
Nothing was left but the ruined Rutledge Inn,
With here and there an excavation which showed
Foundation stones. There facing the sun-lit west
One heard the meadow-lark, or the cawing crow,
And all was silent as the evening glow,
Which somehow beckoned the never quiet quest.

We drove from Petersburg in a carriage hired
At "Birdie" Meyers's main street livery.
And as we drove the robins quired
Along wheat fields and fields of greenery.
Once Herndon went with us, and frequently
Shack Dye, or "Nigger" Dick, the Bennett boys,
Their father, too, the genial Theodore
For years at Petersburg the circuit clerk,
Who loved my father, and such simple joys

As fishing from the dam, or from the shore,
Till the water darkened as the sky grew dark.

That old mill in those days was like a roof,
Or castle prisoned in a crystal glass,
There by the river, separate and aloof
A thing of magic sphered in chrysoprase.
There was no sound about but birds, the rush
Of water from the dam, and now and then
The chuckle of a wagon. The enveloping hush
Seemed like the presence of departed men,
The villagers, like Kelso, Justice Green,
Or Mentor Graham, revisiting the scene
Where once the fears and hopes of life had been.

The vacancy where the mill was is like a wound
Which shows its depth by showing where it healed.
The mill is like a memory marooned
Upon an island of air, by air concealed.
It is a heart-break to no heart revealed,
Save those who knew it when the waters wheeled
The shafts and burrs
For farmers and for villagers.

Ballade of Salem Town

Where is the inn of Salem Town
    Where Lincoln loafed ere we knew his name?
When the Clarys from Prairie Grove were down,
    And he kindled mirth with his wit like flame.
    Loud are these things on the lips of fame,
But crumbled to dust is the log-wood wall,
    And perished alike are 'squire and dame—
The toiling year is the Lord of all.

Where is the mill of such renown?
    And the sluice where the swirling waters came?
And the hamlet's sage and the rustic clown
    And those who had glory and those who had shame?
    And those who lost in this curious game;
The bully, the acred-lord and his thrall—
    Gone are they all beyond Time's reclaim—
The toiling year is the Lord of all.

But when jest passed 'twixt laggard and lown
    And the cold wind whined at the window frame,
Then careless alike of smile or frown
    He builded for those who should carp or blame,
    Thereafter when Error should seek to maim
The hand of Liberty in her hall,
    When he made Malice and Treason tame—
The toiling year is the Lord of all.

Envoy

Prince! this shaft of marble is brown
    Ere a cycle is past, and at last will fall
But fame has fashioned his fadeless crown
    The toiling year is the Lord of all.

New Salem Hill

Flower of Virginia, from which the seed
Sown in Kentucky and Tennessee,
Was carried to this congenial soil
By the Sangamon River on this Hill
Bounded by forests and prairies, so this breed
Of men came here, and as a vigorous clan
Stamped life here with their life and will,
As woodsmen, plowmen, men of toil.
They were earth-people, original and free,
And from their inward life as primitive men
Endowed a landscape with dialects and tales,
And a music which in memory echoes still.

Then from this Sangamon shore,
Not destined as a village to remain,
They wandered soon. And as before
The winds blew, but as the only voices here,
Whining like wounded beasts in pain;
Or roaring from the river valley in gales
Through russet oak leaves whispering and sere.
And crows and wolves from hiding places came,
And perched or skulked where the ruin stood
Of the grocery store, the blacksmith shed,
Or in the dismantled frame
Of the school house; or where the dead
Lay by the regrowing thicket and the wood;
Or in the Tavern where the wind-battered door
Showed the black fireplace with its hollow stare.
And all around were the log huts fallen down
With riven roofs and crumbling chinks

Amid decay as still as falling soot.
A people had passed! New Salem town
Heard the leaves rustle to the rabbit's foot,
And the lisping sound
Of squirrels and gliding minks.

New Salem as a poplar tree had thrived,
And aged too soon and died.
The three-faced camp, the hut of logs
With puncheon floor, and chimney contrived
Of mud, small sticks; the log school house,
The water mill by the river's side;
The mould-board, shovel, and bull-tongue plows,
The hunter with his hunting dogs,
Vanished away, and left a moon-haunted hill,
A soaring headland of trees,
Enchanted by the re-remembered stars,
To lapse to prairie dreams again
Amid autumnal wind and winter rain,
Rending the rumpled roof, the wasting sill.
Gone then the cooper shop, the tannery.
The wheelwright, blacksmith, the village school,
The justice court were seen no more.
And overgrown was the trodden place
Where men played horseshoes, or came to race.
No more upon his smooth, worn stool
The saddler sat. No more by night or afternoon
Men gathered at Berry's Store to chaff
About the week's events, to talk and laugh
Of Clary's Grove, which in their idiom
Was the world to them,
Beyond which was no world at all;
They met no more to dance the fiddle tune,
To wrestle on the grass,
To gossip by the moon,
To drink the friendly glass.
No more the husking bee, the apple festival.
No more to the Tavern table came
Rough-handed men, noisy with merriment
In blue jeans, linsey-woolsey dressed.
Nor in the evening by the Tavern fire

Was there rejoicing that Jackson had restored
By his will and the people's word
The usury-bitten rights of the common man,
And given woodsmen, plowmen, their worthy hire,
And the soil its rulership by the plan
Of Nature and the faith American.
No more by the hearth, which cast a bloom
Over the humble living room,
Was seen the family: the father bent
On making shoes, the mother at the loom,
The daughter at the wheel,
Which whirred its musical content,
While simmered on the crane the evening meal.

Before the Rutledge Tavern on the green
The dancers came as the rising moon
Soared from the river's coolness where the woods
Were deep in shadows strewn,
Like memories falling in revisited solitudes.
The fiddle here woke echoes sweet and keen,
Piercing the forest's hush, which else was still,
Save for the chanting of the whippoorwill,
And save for voices happy and murmurous
About the streets, by doorways; while the East
By soundless wings of light was fanned,
Which wafted an aureole more luminous
As the moon's less timid step released
The doors of the sky with aweless hand.
Those dancers gone, the eddying leaves,
With light from heaven twined,
Danced to the fiddles of the wind.
And when the sun, like tranquil thought,
Like flaming life to death resigned,
Set on the prairie, and New Salem Hill
With silence and long level light was caught;
And when this life-deserted tavern hall
Stood silent and leaning, still
Soared up the moon, but only to enthrall
The ruin of a happiness with her glance
Upon hushed woods, and hearth stones cast
About the broken floor,

Upon the windowless window, and the door
With dumb and open mouth, speaking a past
Of laughter, the fiddle, and the dance

Here on this Hill to blossom burst
A life all new, all pure American.
In western soil this seed of our loveliest flower,
Grown in Virginia first,
And on this Hill re-sown, produced the men
Made altogether of our original earth,
Being close to a soil whose power
Fed their diverging veins.
This Hill is loved, by history is revered
Because America sees its happiest strains
Of a people new, who briefly here appeared,
Simple and virile, joyous, brave, and free,
Kindly, industrious, full of hardihood,
And happy in a sylvan democracy,
And purged of Old World blood.
This woodland flower cut down by drouth and frost,
To cultivated blossoming was lost;
It faded with New Salem Town.
This Bethlehem of America, this shrine
Of a vision vanished, a people passed away,
Is loved because America here beholds
With adoration a freedom and a day
Which dawned and perished when it made the sign
Of what the land should be, and by what moulds
Its spirit needed fashioning.

Through longing for the pastoral loveliness
Of an idyllic past, America looks back
To New Salem on the Hill;
And, loving that vanished people, bestows
On Lincoln its substituting tenderness,
Its reverent love,
Dreaming that he arose
From this people and this scene, a soul thereof.
Hunger of heart to scatter and fulfill
The seed of that village bloom
From sea to sea till the land should all become

The strength, the joy, the freedom, the friendliness,
The liberty, humanity, and good will
Once here, makes this far day remember
New Salem on the Hill.
For if Lincoln had grown
From wise New York, or cold New England, deprived
Of the nurture and the background of these men,
And this village, living as none ever lived,
He would be shorn of soil
To feed the roots of a patriarch name,
And left to stand for what he was alone.
As in his youth of loneliness and need
New Salem fed him, so
The memories of this Hill and people feed
His fabulous fame.
And love for Lincoln is disguised
Love for New Salem eternalized.
For this village of the Western Land,
Blooming in men's spirits now from shore to shore,
And ever more beloved, more memorable,
Was the blossom toward which his hand
Strayed, as if Fate had grown it for
His brow-concealing coronal;
As if Fate meant its fragrance to sanctify
The blood of a merchants' war,
And a people's agony;
Even though armed strife and battle renown
Poisoned the land, never to breed again
Such men of peace, such hearty men,
Or save New Salem Town.

Squire Bowling Green

(Rutledge's Tavern, New Salem, July 14th, 1839.)

You missed it—case all over! Lincoln's gone.
He's just had time about to reach the mill.
He couldn't wait until the stage arrived.
Had business in the courts of Springfield—well,
You can believe he has become a lawyer.
He borrowed Mentor Graham's horse to ride.
John Yoakum is in Springfield and to-morrow
Will bring it back.

          Who won the case? Why, Abe.
He won it by his horse-sense and his wit.
You must have met the jury down the road.
What were they laughing at? About the case.
We started yesterday on the evidence
And finished up this morning. An appeal?
The verdict satisfies both parties, and
My judgment stands.

          Abe is a natural lawyer,
Knows things that can't be found in books, although
He knows the books. And why not? You recall
When he was boarding with me how he studied?
It's just four years ago or so, that he
Came home one night with Blackstone. Well, I've noticed
A man attracts what's his, just like a magnet
Draws bits of steel. You can't make me believe
That Blackstone came to him unless 'twas meant
That he should be a lawyer. Don't you know?

He read this Blackstone in his store all day
And half the night as well. He said to me
Not Volney's "Ruins," Shakespeare, Burns, had taken
His interest like this Blackstone. Yes, he took it
When he went fishing with Jack Kelso, read,
And let Jack row the boat and bait the hooks. . . .

I think he knows this Blackstone all by heart.
But anyway, he knows the human heart.
Well, now here is the case: Here is a colt.
George Cameron says the colt is his—John Spears
Says no, the colt is mine, and Cameron sues,
And Spears defends, and sixty witnesses
Come here to testify, on my word it's true,
On my judicial oath it is the fact.
The thirty swear the colt is Cameron's;
And thirty swear the colt belongs to Spears;
And not a man impeached, these witnesses
And everyone good men, and most of them
I know as I know you. Well, what's to do?
The scales are balanced. And besides all this,
Here's Cameron who swears the colt is his,
And Spears who swears the opposite, and both
Are credible, I know them both. So I
Sit like a fellow trying to decide
What happens when a thing impenetrable
Is struck by something irresistible—
I'm stumped, that's all.

                    You see the facts were these:
Each of these fellows owns a mare, the mares
Look pretty much alike, each had a colt
In April. But the other day one colt—
Which colt, that is the question—strayed away
And can't be found. George Cameron has a colt—
These men are neighbors—but John Spears comes over
And sees the colt at Cameron's in the field;
And says, "That is my colt." "Not on your life,"
George Cameron replies, "The colt is mine—
Your colt has strayed, not mine." They come to law.
John Spears gets Lincoln, and they come to court

With sixty witnesses; and here this noon
With all the evidence put in, I sit
And eye the jury, know the jury's stumped,
As I am stumped.

Then Lincoln says: "Your honor,
Let's have a trial on view." I'd heard of that,
But never sat on such a trial before.
"Let's bring the colt, the two mares over here,
And let the jury see which mare the colt
Resembles, let the jury use their eyes
As witnesses use theirs."

That seemed fair.
And so we sent one fellow for the mares,
Another for the colt. For Lincoln said:
"Your honor, bring them separate, so the jury
Can have the sudden flash of seeing them
Separate, to study them."

For an hour
Abe sat here in the shade and told us stories.
And pretty soon we heard the horses whinney,
And heard the colt. And Lincoln said, "Your honor,
Let's have the mares led past the jury, trotting,
Let's see their pace." And so they trotted them.
"Now trot the colt," said Lincoln—we did that.
The jury watched to see the look of legs,
And movement, if you please, to catch a likeness.
But nothing came of this. Then Lincoln said:
"Now turn the colt loose"—and they turned it loose.
It galloped to the mare of Spears and sucked!
Well, now it's true a colt's a silly thing,
And may mistake its mother, but a mare
Will never let a colt that's not her own
Put under flanks its nose. Of course the jury,
And all of us know that—and so did Abe.
The jury yelled and all the witnesses
Began to whoop. And when I rapped for order
And got things quiet—Lincoln rose and said,
"I rest, your honor."

So I entered judgment
For Spears. They went to Berry's for the drinks—
There! hear them laughing.

Lincoln took his fee,
Ten dollars, I believe, and went to Springfield.

Achilles Deatheridge

"Your name is Achilles Deatheridge?
How old are you, my boy?"
"I'm sixteen past and I went to the war
From Athens, Illinois."

"Achilles Deatheridge, you have done
A deed of dreadful note."
"It comes of his wearing a battered hat,
And a rusty, wrinkled coat."

"Why didn't you know how plain he is?
And didn't you ever hear,
He goes through the lines by day or night
Like a sooty cannoneer?"

"You must have been half dead for sleep,
For the dawn was growing bright."
"Well, Captain, I had stood right there
Since six o'clock last night."

"I cocked my gun at the swish of the grass
And how am I at fault
When a dangerous looking man won't stop
When a sentry hollers halt?"

"I cried out halt and he only smiled
And waved his hand like that.
Why, any Johnnie could wear the coat
And any fellow the hat."

"I hollered halt again and he stopped
And lighted a fresh cigar.
I never noticed his shoulder badge,
And I never noticed a star."

"So you arrested him? Well, Achilles,
When you hear the swish of the grass
If it's General Grant inspecting the lines
Hereafter let him pass."

Memorabilia

Old pioneers, how fare your souls to-day?
They seem to be
Imminent about this pastoral way,
This sunny lea.
The elms and oaks you knew, greenly renew
Their leaves each spring,
But never comes the hour again which drew
Your world from view.

Here in a mood I lay, deep in the grass,
Between the graves;
And saw ye rise, ye shadowy forms, and pass
O'er the wind's waves;
Sunk eyes and bended head, wherefrom is fled
The light of life;
Even as the land, whose early youth is dead,
Whose glory fled.

With eighty years gone over what remains
For tongue to tell?
Hence was it that in silence, with no pains
At last 'twas well,
Under these trees to creep, for ultimate sleep
To soothe regret,
For the world's ways, for war, let mankind reap,
You said, and weep.

Abram Rutledge died, ere the great war
Ruined the land.
His well-loved son was struck on fields afar

By a brother's hand.
Then brought they him, O pioneer, on his bier
To the hill and the tree,
Back home and laid him, son of Trenton, here
Your own grave near.

Of all unuttered griefs, of vaguest woes,
None equals this:
Forgotten hands, and work that no one knows
Whose work it is;
Good gifts bequeathed, but never earned, or spurned
In hate or pride;
And the boon of an age destroyed, ere a cycle turned
O'er you inurned.

Abram Rutledge lies in a sunken grave,
Dust and no more,
Let Freedom fail, it is naught to him, who was brave,
Who stood to the fore.
The oaks and elms he knew, greenly renew
Their leaves each spring,
But gone his dream with that last hour which drew
His world from view.

Concord Church

For years it stood in lonelihood
Upon this rise of ground,
Abandoned to this solitude
Of fields without a sound;
With flapping doors, and benches strewed,
And shutters sagged and browned.

Flitting through holes the swallows made
Nests in the chandeliers.
A tree grew through the roof and spread
Its branches through the years.
And field-mice under the platform bred,
Where sat the pioneers.

The figured paper from the wall
By winter winds was stripped.
The organ long unmusical
From the pulpit place was tipped.
The stoves and pipes were left to fall
In cinders water-dripped.

From hymn books many a rifled sheet
Went rustling night and day.
Beside the broken Mercy Seat
The toppled pulpit lay;
And rats made nests for their retreat
Where men once knelt to pray.

The winds whined through the broken panes,
And flapped the carpet loose,

And through the roof the winter rains
Poured down upon the pews.
And dust, debris, and weather stains
Came on its long disuse.

And never a hill by midnights still
Grew lonelier or more weird,
When the door creaked on the broken sill,
And the vacant windows peered;
When the stars kept watch on the graves until
The moon from the prairie neared;

When from afar was a rooster's crow
And the bay of a hound near by,
Then Concord Church was a skeleton woe
Under the midnight's sky;
And through a cornice rift the glow
Of a star burned like an eye.

But Concord Church was built to prove
That every soul is saved
Which rests its hope on Jesus' love,
And none is God-depraved.
And long ago it rose and throve,
And Calvin's hatred braved.

And for a hundred years it went
Against the Calvin breed;
And all the while was blandishment;
But nothing could succeed
To win it from its old dissent,
And from its loving creed.

Nothing availed till Calvin craft
The high assembly fooled;
And then this country church was graffed
To the city bole that ruled
Through Calvin, only to feel the haft
With its life-blood lopped and cooled.

Nothing availed till Calvin's men
Got title by law and fraud

To Concord Church to rule again
Its flock so long abroad.
Its door was closed then, it was then
Its people were outlawed.

Its door to heaven then was barred
To those who loved its truth.
They would not enter who had warred
Upon it with claw and tooth;
Nor suffer those who had regard
For its entrance sweet and smooth.

The farmer folk could not withstand
The Calvin gold and power.
And Calvin's ghost made contraband
This pulpit from that hour.
And thus the church door being banned
Went flapping to wind and shower.

The pulpit Bible, as it were pitched
By an earthquake to the floor,
Lay through the years and grew unstitched;
And all the four walls bore
A look as if they were bewitched
From what they were before.

And thus the churchyard overgrown
With briers, weeds, and vines
Left the dead pioneer unknown;
For how could there be shrines
When mourners were debarred, or gone
Where daylight never shines?

The time came when the sons of sons
No longer lived, while those
Thrice still removed, as memory runs,
Know not the church arose
To teach that heaven's benisons
No grace of heaven oppose.

Who was John Clary who died the noon

Fort Sumter saw the fire?
Who was the Pantier, friend of Boone,
That Revolutionary sire?
Who were these Houghtons, Engels strewn
Mid milk-weed, thistle, brier?

Who was the Reverend Goodpasture
Who preached here sixty years?
Who were these children of the poor?
These long dead pioneers?
Why let these rotting walls endure,
Which no one now reveres?

The faith these churches held is dead,
The congregation gone.
This ruin on its pillars spread
Will soon collapse thereon;
This hill has better use, they said,
Than for this skeleton.

They tore it down, and left no trace
Of what so long had stood.
They left no scantlin, shingle, brace,
Nor sills by axes hewed.
They left the fence alone to face
The churchyard's solitude,

Through which stray hogs and cattle pass
Upon the graves to browse;
And where the black snake through the grass
Glides for the scampering mouse;
And where ere long the tangled mass
Will be torn up with plows.

Thus, as before the church was raised,
Stands now the lonely hill.
Afar the prairie land is blazed
By sunsets strangely still.
By night the Concord Creek is hazed
Where sings the whippoorwill.

The moon comes forth above the vale,
And over it springs the sun.
And from the pastures cry the quail,
And men their courses run,
While Concord Church has told its tale,
Which is oblivion.

At night the sky-space over the hill,
Which the vanished church makes bare,
Is an arc of eternity with the chill
And presence of breathless air;
It is not love, nor good, nor ill
But the infinite brooding there.

It is a calm and lidless brow
At the far horizon's rim
Which says there is not then nor now,
Nor grief if Time bedim
The preacher's name, nor if the plow
Unearth him limb by limb.

For Reverend Goodpasture has been
These fifty years forgot,
Who drew away from John Calvin,
Nor saw the earth was not
Compassionate to men wherein
Their heartache finds its lot.

Nor studied the cruel stars of Time;
Nor how all things devour
Whatever helps to crawl or climb;
And how life is a flower
Cut down by hungry scythes or rime
Amid its loveliest hour.

The soaring sky will never let
Life's love, or truth, or search,
Or faith live, save the amulet
Of gold keep off the smirch,
The loss and vanishment which beset
The walls of Concord Church.

The Old Farm

At last not only to men do age and change
Descend, but also to the spot
We knew they come with hands to blot
What was, and make it strange.

The old beloved house by fire or frost
Goes down, the orchard perishes;
Beyond, the forest vanishes,
And the road is fenced and lost.

There are new boundaries; the hedges pass;
And with the neighbor houses gone
The landscape is a scene whereon
One looks to find the grass

The only thing unchanged, save the far hills,
Albeit shrunk, the eternal clouds
Above them, made wind-woven shrouds
For the day; or the plaintive shrills

Of the enduring wind; or the lark's sad breast;
Which has no memory of Springs
We knew, nor of ancestral wings
Which once this sky possessed;

Nor recks our memories of the distant year
Of the ploughman's voice at break of day
On Shipley's Hill; or far away
The dinner bell of Spears.

We standing here reflect upon this land
About, or that from sea to sea
Which took them when they ceased to be,
Who once these meadows manned;

Who as the Benson boys and William Shultz
From weary year to weary year
Toiled for the corn, whose humble sphere
Was soil of the earth, which rules

Man's life, and covers him with oblivion
When all his labor has been spent,
And all his grief and merriment
Are passed away and done.

Yet clouds still sail over the Sangamon shore.
But where's the road of that July
We drove our wagon to come by
The mouth of the Lattimore?

If in that night of thunder, rain, and flame
We two had perished in our camp,
Long since our places and the stamp
Of our faces, and our name

Had gone from Time, as they must go, despite
The long years we have lived since then
Of labor, change, and vanished men,
Of hopes and lost delight.

Not even a trace remains of your father's house,
My grandsire's, nor the path he paced;
Naught of the orchard trees which faced
The spot of maple boughs,

Where that old couple, like ancient Philemon
And Baucis, sat so many years
Outwatching life as pioneers,
Till all of life was gone;

With scarcely a voice their annals to commend,
Their neighbor life, their days' routine;
And gone long since that William Greene,
Your father's life-time friend.

Have we survived for something? Ask the plain,
Or the Mason county hills afar,
Whose earth will be our sepulchre.
Whether 'twas loss or gain!

Old Georgie Kirby

Old Georgie Kirby who for forty years has lain
Beneath this sky, amid this boundless pasture,
    With rich blue grass for vesture,
His curses ended against the ruinous rain
Which drowned his bottom land, and spoiled his corn,
Was brought to nothingness, as quiet
As the sky above, the fiat
Which made no answer to his blasphemous scorn.

For when the rain came and his corn was drowned
He stood and shook his fist against high heaven,
    He mocked the violet levin,
He pitched his curses against the thunder's sound.

Defying God he said, "In ancient days
You drowned the world, do it again, old devil,
    And make these hollows level
With water to the hills, blot out the ways
And roads to town, throw open windows, doors
In your revengeful sky, and wreck my labor,
And flash your lightning's sabre—
God damn it, I don't care now how it pours."

His pious neighbor, old Nathaniel Page,
Expected Georgie to be struck by lightning
    For blasphemy so frightening.
But Georgie lived to eighty years of age.
He lived to bury wife and every child,
And build this picket fence here in the meadow

Around their graves, on which the shadow
Of hawk and crow floats from the sky reviled.

Nathaniel Page himself has reached no peace
Greater than Georgie's in this silent prairie,
Here in this cemetery,
Though rain falls and deep thunder stirs the trees,
And rumbles the hills, and shakes what bones remain
Of Georgie, cursing no more the lightning, thunder,
And flooded fields; himself thereunder
Is a fellow worker now with storm and rain.

Nathaniel Page

Nathaniel Page loved God with soul dissolved
In gospel love. He thought his own transgression
      Brought flood and rust and Hessian
Flies on his crops, and so his heart resolved
A deeper penitence, a faith contrite
Before the Awful Power, which ever brooded
Over the prairie, changeful mooded
As thunder clouds, again as summer light.

A cyclone in the night that passed around
The house of Georgie Kirby with no ravage
      Smote Page's like a savage,
And laid his barn and corn-cribs to the ground.
Old Georgie laughed and swore, Nathaniel prayed,
And searched his soul for evil,
      Believing that the devil
Was sent by God for heaven disobeyed.

Six miles of sky divide the several graves
Of these two men, Page's is in the village,
      Georgie's is where the tillage
Still takes the flood, and where the winter raves,
And where the wind drives over the lonely plain.
Under six miles of sky you ponder
      Their God-mood, as you wander
Down hills, by woodlands and through Bowman's Lane.

The Mourner's Bench

They're holding a revival at New Hope Meeting house,
I can't keep from going, I ought to stay away.
For I come home and toss in bed till day,
For thinking of my sin, and the trouble I am in.
I dream I hear the dancers
In the steps and swings,
The quadrilles and the lancers
They danced at Revis Springs.
I lie and think of Charley, Charley, Charley
The Bobtown dandy
Who had his way with me.
And no one is so handy
A dancer as Charley
To Little Drops of Brandy,
Or the Wind that Shakes the Barley,
Or Good mornin' Uncle Johnny I've fetched your Wagon Home.

And Greenberry Atterberry, who toed it like a pigeon
Has gone and got religion;
He's deserted the dancers, the fiddlers, merry-makers,
And I should do it too.
For Charley, Charley has left me for to roam.
But a woman at the mourner's bench must tell her story true —
What shall I do? What shall I do?

My grandmother told me of Old Peter Cartwright
Who preached hell-fire
And the worm that never dies.
And here's a young preacher at the New Hope Meeting house,

And every one allows, he has old Peter's brows,
And flaming of the eyes,
And the very same way, they say.
Last night he stuck his finger right down in my direction,
And said: "God doesn't care
For your woman's hair.
Jesus wants to know if your soul is fair
As your woman's complexion."
And then I thought he knew—
O what shall I do?

Greenberry Atterberry, weeping and unsteady
Had left his seat already.
He stood at the mourner's bench in great tribulation
And told the congregation:
That fiddling and dancing and tobacco chewin'
Led up to whisky and to woman's ruin—
And I thought he looked at me.

Well, you can stop dancing, and you can stop drinking
And you can leave the quarter-horses at the crooked races.
But a woman, a woman, the people will be thinking
Forever of a woman who confesses her behavior.
And then I couldn't look in the people's faces,
All weeping and singing, O gentle Saviour!
Then the devil said: You wench
You'd cut a pretty figure at the mourner's bench,
Go out and look for Charley,
Go out and look for Charley,
He's down at Leese's Grove.
He has found a fresh love
Go win him back again.
He is dancing on the platform to the Speckled Hen.

O Saviour, Saviour, how can I join the mourners,
Face all the scorners?
But how can I hunt Charley at Leese's Grove?
How can I stand the staring, the whispering of things
Down at Revis Springs?
How can I stand the mocking of the fiddle strings?

Charley! Charley!
So it's knowing what's best to do,
Saviour! Saviour!
Its knowing what's best to do!

Bill Schultz

Was it for self, for wife and children only
That Bill Schultz toiled the years through, and at morn
Arose to drive the plow, here in this lonely
    Land of the corn?

Was all his patience, labor, sense of duty
Spent for a roof, for bread, and none remained
As treasure here or somewhere, for a beauty
    That life has gained?

For otherwise, now that his days are ended,
And grass is over him, and there's no more to say,
Would it much matter if his steps had wended
    Some selfish way?

For what was all day in the meadow mowing?
For what the humble supper, the early bed?
For what the early rising to be sowing,
    If just for bread?

And the long winters when his brood was huddled
About the fire, while he amid the snow
Was feeding cattle for cities life-befuddled—
    I'd like to know?

If he means this, and nothing more, nor quickens
Anything for him, save a pang like mine,
The life of ants, of crickets, or of chickens
    Is just as fine.

I don't know why it is, but in strange places,
Like Egypt, to my fancy he was shown.
A peasant's song in France mid alien faces
    Seemed like his own.

At night sometimes when wakefulness is bringing
Remembrance, then I see him with his plow
On Shipley's Hill, and I can hear him singing
    So plain, somehow.

And then I think how fifty years of labor
Availed him — what? And how he earned and lost
A little farm; and how he joined his neighbor
    For California's coast,

After his wife had died, that El Dorado
Of hopeful men, whom life has spent or crushed;
And then I think how soon he found the shadow
    Of silent dust.

Was it for self, for wife, for children, duty
That Bill Schultz toiled? Or was it just to give
To Shipley's Hill a memory and a beauty
    To us who live?

Shipley Corn-Crib

Aloft on Shipley's Hill against blue skies
The corn-crib is like an agate square
Sunk in turquoise, as if it would declare
The heaven above and earth of mysteries.
But far above, on high, but far away
The sky spreads, and beyond the river stretches
Where fabled farms and houses brood,
Under a light that etches
The slopes and fields, the distant wood,
Where day becomes too pale for day.

Yet this corn-crib is lonely and seems to feel
The vastness of the sky, it seems
To the unnamed Something to appeal
With longing, with memorial dreams.
Across the road is the weed-grown yard
Where plowmen, children of the school were buried,
So long forgotten, even of perished names,
Who have no more the neighborhood's regard.
They to this sky, where now no cloud is flurried,
Reprove all wars, all strife, all fames.

And to the north, using the old field-glass
I can discern the grave-yard, stones and fence
Of Georgie Kirby, exiled amid the grass.
This too is under the vast omnipotence
Of the sky that bends above the Shipley Hill,
The corn-crib. Look no farther for a scene
That will stay thought and waken pain,
Or stir a wonder in the mind or fill

The heart with longing for what has been,
And will not be again.

No longer look for landscapes which suggest
The mystery of man in this strange sphere;
The Shipley corn-crib standing here
Fills full the breast
With wonder that conquers fear.

Going to Atterberry

Over to Atterberry, ambling to the West,
You can see the church's spire miles and miles away.
Over to Charley Clary's store, that's our morning quest,
Underneath thc bluest skies on an April day.
How our horses plod along on this plastic dirt;
Yielding to their hoofs like a rubber spring;
How our stirrup straps swing, how the prairies skirt
For miles and miles about us, how the blackbirds sing,

Where the larks soar, where the pools bright with water stand,
Rimmed with flags that whisper to the wandering wind,
Where the corn begins to sprout, all around the land,
Where the rail fence with flowering vines all are intertwined.
How our horses crunch their bits, how our saddles creak,
How the wind is in our ears like a murmuring shell.
Passing Doggie Dawson we rein up to speak—
On we go again past where the Engels dwell.

Into Atterberry, our horses in a trot,
We come at last and tie up, happy to be where
Fishing lines and hooks are, so we cross the lot,
And enter where the smell of jeans and leather fills the air.
And there is Charley Clary, happy with red cheeks,
Who greets us with a hearty laugh, and talks about the crops.
Pretty soon the train comes, as the whistle shrieks
We hurry to the platform where the engine stops.

With all our fishing tackle, with needles and with thread,
With hinges, nails, tobacco we mount our horses now.
Again the cushioned thumping of their punctuated tread,

We hurry home for dinner, this afternoon to plow.
The forests rim about us, the prairie grasses bend,
The larks soar up, the blackbirds warble ecstasies.
This is an April prairie where everyone's a friend,
This is a land of sunshine, of plenty and of peace.

To the south at Concord soldiers lie in sleep
Forgetful of the war done, and of the wars to come.
The world may roar with slaughter, armies die like sheep,
Here the crows are calling, here the wild bees hum.
Give us but an hour for riding to the village,
Give us but an hour of laughter as we ride,
That can wall away the battles and their pillage,
We can snatch a happiness whatever may betide.

New Hope Meetinghouse

My heart is full of sorrow over New Hope Meetinghouse,
It burned down so long ago it's now all forgot,
And weeds and corn are growing in the old-time spot
Where the folks once stood about, and talked when church
    was out.
I keep thinking of the people
By horse and shank's mare
Who assembled at this steeple
For singing and for prayer.
I seem to hear voices, voices, voices
Of the farmer congregation
When every eye was dim;
And the sorrow of salvation
Was a sorrow that rejoices;
And faith and its foundation,
And the soul's consecration
Were nothing but the singing of a gospel hymn.

The souls of that people were their own Holy Scriptures,
And they searched them by their singing, and instead of
    puzzle pictures
Of the Bible, they had song.
The mood that moved their singing was their test of right and
    wrong;
The creed was love and heaven, and the sweet forget-me-nots,
The poetry of Wesley, of Cowper and of Watts;
The faith was give the poor man, the humble man his due,
And make a neighbor in your heart of everyone you knew.

I never shall forget the eyes of old grandmothers

Who looked at me so tenderly
In their faded hats and cloaks;
Or Greenberry Atterberry whose voice with feeling trembled
When calling me a good lad
Because he loved my folks.
I still can hear their voices as they sang of love excelling,
Of rocks and hills and valleys where milk and honey flowed;
And how beyond the Jordan was a fair eternal dwelling
Where the heart would find its happiness,
And the soul an abode.
This is the Word as mystical as the coal borne by the
    seraphims,
Some seed was from the Bible, but their hearts were the soil;
It was a flower of human love,
Of man love and woman love,
A separate religion made of hymns.

And now amid the hammer's blow, the squawking of the radio,
The rattle of the trucks on the walls along the street,
I hear their singing voices above the iron noises,
I see the grove of oak trees, and endless fields of wheat.
Before me come the faces of old Malkom Hubley,
Of old Samuel Blivens, of old George Spear,
Just as I saw them as a boy assembled for the very joy
Of singing of a heaven that shortly would appear;
Singing with their women and their children of a happy land,
The far away home of the soul beyond the flood;
Singing, soon the light of day
Shall forever pass away,
Singing of the fountain filled with blood.

And though it may have been that some debated sin,
And the fate that man was in;
And if some were soul-concerned
For salvation to be earned,
Not eternally decreed,
All of this is past and gone,
And their singing long was blown
Far away along the blast
That destroyed that simple past;
Scarcely memory remains

How they trebled forth the strains
Of the hymns by poets framed
All the centuries along,
How their spirits rose and flamed
In their song.

Where are the bones of old Elvira Momeyer,
Where are the skulls of old man Smoot,
Old man Craig, and old man Alkire,
Old John McNamar and Parthenia Clute?
Where, since the graveyard of the New Hope Meetinghouse
Was plowed up and harrowed and planted in corn?
Where, since they closed their eyes in hope of a paradise
Welcomed by hymns at the resurrection morn?

O Orphics, Orphics of the Illinois prairies,
Of Goodpastures, Clarys!
O voice of Royal Potter whose thundering tones
Overflowed the church as a goblet which brims,
In singing the hymns
In deep crescendos and quavering whims!
O Royal Potter, O Royal Potter
What has become of your venerable skull,
Your resurrection bones,
Your judgment day bones and skull?

Kildeer

Down through the blue-grass, running in long billows,
Heaped by the west wind, past the Lattimore,
Bordered by cattails, by the green willows,
Under a sky where white clouds soar;
Down to the pasture pond, by the lush morasses,
Beyond the nodding clover—
Then suddenly a cry, a flutter from the grasses—
Upsprings the startled plover,
Crying "kildeer," "kildeer," with wings interweaving,
Making parentheses against the open sky,
Voice of the June hours, for the April grieving,
Soaring and dipping, lost to the eye

Fellow to the winds, and to the green flags kindred,
Messenger of the prairie, and spirit of the hills,
Lost in the levels, hastening unhindered,
Soul of the landscape, heart that mourns and trills.
What a lonely melody, speaking the pioneer,
Winged grief that startles, and dies far away;
When his wings have vanished still you hear "kildeer"
Over dimming acres where the sky is gray.

Corn in the Shock: Menard County

This russet hill, oak-crowned, beside the road
That upward winds, is tented with tepees
Of summer hours, which speak of absentees
Who crossed the river where summer still abode.
This sixty acre patch toward the west,
Where stands the school house, is a camp forlorn,
So filled is it with wigwams of the corn,
Whose treasures by the crib are now possessed.

The wire on the fence posts winds and sags;
A silo by a barn is like a butte
In the desert country, and would break the mute
Trance of its contemplation. Rakes and drags
Litter the barnyard. And afar the fans
Of a windmill pause, thoughtful and motionless;
Above a herd of cattle cropping cress;
By the porch of the farm house are the empty cans

For milk, and on the porch's wall are hung
Old coats and dippers, tools. Strainers and churns
Stand by the door. Until the wife returns
They will be silent. They will find a tongue
At milking time. She will not stand and count
The prairie barns and houses, nor survey
Those miles of wigwams in the fading day,
Which dip with swales and with the uplands mount.

But the moon will lure her. Still she has rapt care
For that slender strip of silver, or if it be
In fullness, to watch that bright immensity

Rise over Shipley's Hill to the upper air,
And shine upon the wigwams and hay ricks,
And the lonely oak tree. If you would find unknown
Secrets, stand by the oak tree all alone,
Where the falling leaf just touches earth and ticks,
Just as a twinkle from the moon is blown.

Not to See Sandridge Again

Amid these city walls I often think
Of Sandridge, and its billowed land between
The woods and hills, where clover, red and pink,
And corn fields, oat fields, wheat fields, gold and green,
Lie under skies of speeding clouds serene,
Where gardens know the robin, bobolink.

The yellow road that travels by the hedge,
The rail fence till it slants the gradual rise
Of farms toward the upland fields that edge
The Sangamon, touched by descending skies—
This, too, I see; this is that loved Sandridge,
All changed, but changeless in my memories.

Orchards and strips of timber, walls of log,
Barns, windmills, creeks, even the Shipley Pond
Have vanished, like the early-morning fog
That hung above the swales, and far beyond
The pastures, where the patient shepherd dog
Followed the farmer, dutiful and fond.

Earth even may change, but if the love it stirs
Remains, is Earth then changed? If man must pass,
And generations of cattle, if harvesters
Themselves are gathered, and old men sink like grass
Into the quiet of the universe,
Yet memory keeps them, they are never less.

That is eternal life for them, for me.
For what is living save it be that what

Was beauty is preserved in memory?
If gazing on a dead face is to blot
What the dead was in life, so not to see
Sandridge again may be the better lot.

In Memory of Alexander Dexter Masters

No heart's sin is more punished than the sin
Of that forgetfulness of a heart which dies.
Beauty and Truth with wide, accusing eyes
Will smite a recreant memory for what has been.

What though the noisy days, the stress of life
Cover the dead? What though the power of thought
Less vividly can summon what is not?
Hours come that bear the knife:

The silence and the uncomplaining lot
Of the dead wound like a sudden strain
Of music, and fill the heart with pain
For loveliness forgot.

In that hot summer fifty years ago
You passed in agony, and I have wandered on
This intervening time, forgetting you were gone
For days, for years—how did I so?

You were a boy miraculous of face,
And you were gifted with ethereal mind.
How strange the Fate that to your heart assigned
Five years of life—and then your vacant place!

And then our tears, the grave, back to the house
Resuming life, and then the passing days,
The years, and change, and living which betrays
For its poor self our wondering brows.

And the long years in which no answers come
To us who ask why you were born to die
So soon—where you departed to, and why
The tomb remains the tomb.

Back in Oakford

What madness entered in my blood that I came back to
    Oakford,
And left Chicago where I lived since when I was a boy?
What dreams come in the tired heart to blind and to destroy,
Then leave that heart alone in a place where all is gone!
The Fates should have some pity
On a man whose life matured
In the byways of the city,
And should have his longings cured
Of visions of his village with its church and elevator,
The corn cribs and the depot,
The train twice a day,
The store where they sold calico,
And shoes and indigo,
And liver-regulator,
And where things could be charged if you lacked the means to
    pay.

How could I have the foolish dreams of rides about the
    country
With Creel Stith, dead these many years,
And Henry Schirding too?
How could I linger lovingly on hours with Thomas Turner,
Who went to Texas years ago,
And then from life withdrew?
How could I fancy festivals and hunts along the river,
And evenings by the kitchen stove with men who sped the
    plow?
What so misled my famished heart for pleasures gone forever,
Because old friends had vanished,

Or got the frosted brow?

What made me leave the city, though it had grown too sterile,
And journey back to Oakford, decayed and so deserted,
And sunk down in a pasture trance, by lonely forests skirted,
With every soul that gave it life for many years away?
Where were my memory and thought forgetting all the peril
Of being again in Oakford where its twenty houses stood,
Just as they did before I left to go up to the city,
But standing as the tombs that marked a deathly solitude?
How did my heart deceive my mind,
In wandering so fond and blind,
In dreaming that what once had been
Would be the same thing now?

So here I am in Oakford, and Chicago is behind me.
Why sit about the grocery store belonging to the chain?
Why go down to the depot, Ben Sutton is no longer there,
No one is there to loaf about and watch the coming train?
There is no one to visit with. My name is but a memory,
My family's name has faded out, my life at last is caught:
I can't go to Chicago and knit the threads of life again,
I sit about and walk about, a being half distraught.
I pass Tom Turner's little house, owned by a dark Sicilian,
I enter at the drug store run by a swarthy Pole,
The harness shop, the blacksmith shop are gone, and there's
    an alien
Who owns the town's garage, and deals in gas and oil.

The fields and meadows torture me, they seem as mouths that
    yawn
Wide as the sky, and call and call
For something that is gone.
The sinking of the sun seems death, and when the shadows
    fall,
The darkness and deep silence, and the loneliness of night
Come down on all the houses. I sit here by my window,
And see by nine or ten o'clock no window with a light.

I sit here in my room alone and hear the radio intone
The voices of Chicago, the music of the dance,

Not wishing for the city, as Oakford wishes not for me,
But thinking what my dreams have done,
And where my dreams have led,
And how I got to Oakford by an angel-devil chance,
By loneliness and dreaming, and their evil necromance,
And how at last I'm mad.

Memories of Pinafore

By low hills through Petersburg winds the Sangamon
Year by year, even as souls come and depart;
Like its waters they are here, they are gone,
Like the blood leaving and returning to the heart.

But we can never forget the loveliness
Of Nettie Robbins, who played the score
For Kate Degge, Theodore Fisher in the dress
Of characters in magical *Pinafore*.

And we must ever think of him
Who rollicked through Dick Deadeye, of her
Who sang her wares to the crew alert and trim,
And made a captain of Ralph, the prisoner.

They live being a higher existence which sprang
From our love; they are the moon,
"Bright regent of the heavens," to which they sang,
As it were the moon itself over the river dune.

They have a world of their own, a miniature
Sphere of crystal, in which we gaze:
This is a deathless world, which will endure,
As the astral soul of perished days.

The echo of music will long survive
The music itself, and those who sleep
On the hills, by *Pinafore* still live
And still their influence keep.

This is immortality standing over
The headstone and the sunken sod,
Partaking of the life of song, the lover,
God who is Beauty, Beauty who is God.

That is the worship that can always find
An altar with its acceptable sacrifice,
The gift of the Eternal Mind
To hearts devoted, wise.

I Shall Never See You Again

If I could only see you again—
If I could only see you again!
How can it be
I shall never see you again?
For the world has shown it can roll on its way
And blot you out forever—
And I shall never see you again!
I thrill as one who slips on the edge of a gulf
When I think I shall never see you again!

As a dead leaf is hurtled over the tops of trees;
As a dead leaf is dizzily driven through woodland valleys
I am driven and tossed in the storms of living.
But as the dead leaf escapes the breeze's fingers,
And sinks till it nestles motionless under a rock
So in quiet moments I dream
Of you,
I dream of all that you were—
And I shall never see you again!

There never was any one like you!
There never yet was such joy in a heart,
Such strength to live whatever the fate,
Such love to love,
Such thought to see how life is good,
Such maternal passion,
Such breasts eager to nurse child after child—
And I shall never see you again!

Your breasts were made to suckle conquerors,
Warriors, prophets,

Invincible souls
Loving life, and loving death at last.
And now your breasts are dust,
You are all dust,
You are lost save for my memory.

And this morning I woke
As a leaf might wake in its sheltered place
Under the rock
Stirred by a breath of April.
And I lived again the last time I saw you—
The last visit!
You were almost ninety then.
But there was the old zest in your heart
To do all things and have all things
Unchanged, as I had known them
As a boy.
You gave me the same room,
Nothing was changed,
Not a chair, a curtain, a picture.
And you came up-stairs before it was day
And lighted a fire in the little stove
To have the room warm for me to dress in—
There never was love like yours!

And I went down to the kitchen and found you
Frying batter cakes, and laughing,
And bringing back my boyhood days
With the old stories.
And how you kissed me, and hugged me
With your withered arms!
And then you sat down with me,
And ate with me as of old,
And brought out priceless jars of things
Which you had made and saved for me!

The breath of memory stirs me
Under the rock.
I must have the madness of life to drive me,
To toss me
Into forgetfulness of my loss of you—
For I shall never see you again!

The Sangamon River

From near Decatur, from Springfield the river twists
To Athens, then to New Salem Hill
    Of the vanished water mill,
Whose outlines, now a ghost of mists
    Will be refilled, replacing
The mill that is gone. Over the ruined dam
    The waters still are racing
To Petersburg, past bluffs, through levels
Of corn land, where still are revels
Of larks that soar the deep sky's oriflam.

Concrete and steel now span
The river at Petersburg, where for many years
The treacherous waters ran
Under a covered bridge with limestone piers.
Then on to Greenview, past Blue Lake, and through
The farms of Traylors, Clarys;
And bending from the north around the prairies
It takes its western way where Sheep's Ford was,
And where brush, logs its ways bestrew,
Making safe rafts for turtles as they pass.
And dead trees on the shore
Of giant elms and sycamore
Stretch up like skeleton hands
As perches for the hawk, whose wings
Seem a draped rag, and there he clings
And broods above the silent lands.
Kay Watkins ferry then, where neither boat,
Nor men to ferry are, but where
A something says to men, "Take note

Whatever happens I will be here."

All the good, beloved people, those
Who drove the plow near the ford of Mussel Shells,
Are gone, and where Charles Garrits lived now grows
Around his hermit door the thicket, and here dwells
In solitary possession the cawing crow,
The water snake, the blacksnake, and the skunk,
As fallen trunk on trunk
Enrich the shore where the muddy waters flow,
And flow until they mingle with the stream
Of the Illinois; while that, as if possessed
By the sorcery of a dream,
Bends to the Mississippi, and it in turn
Obeys the Gulf, and that the sea—
All waters and all souls forever yearn
For the deep secret of eternity.

An Old County History

Upon the faces of Aunt Sally Short,
Judge Clark and Isaac Scott,
Parthena Green and Dr. Cort,
Samuel Hall and William Nott
Long looking, in this county history shown,
People I knew in boyhood and when grown,
For a moment surprise took hold of me
Casting their ages up if they were alive.
All would be over a hundred, one would be
A hundred and ten, and two a hundred and five.
These twenty years and more they ceased to strive;
Long have they known the change of grass and tree.

The soul's immortal as the heart recalls
Its love for people such as these,
And blots the mind's thought which lists animals
And men together by like biologies.
The heart says, "Dear Aunt Sally, you must dwell,
All of you of such tender pieties,
In heaven with the Lamb where all is well,
By glittering strands, and valleys of pure delight."
But the mind mocks and says, "Incredible;
Aunt Sally's beginning was a single cell;
Began Judge Clark, too, as a micro-mite;
To all of them this origin befell.
How then the beautiful land, the infinite bliss,
The Lamb from such a simple genesis?"

Born like the swallows or the swine,
Judge Clark and Isaac Scott,

Aunt Sally and Parthena Green
Made houses and left memory sweet as wine.
Up from invisible life their strength begot
The beauty of a neighborhood and a scene
Of pioneer truth upon their chosen spot.
If from this something made they shall increase
By some progression to larger happiness,
The wonder is neither more nor less;
But if they are the sport of some caprice,
What need have they of pity or redress
Having the meadow's peace?

The Night Watch

How is it, Edwin, that you humbly live
In dingy rooms like these, this street
Is dingy, too, and seems unmeet
For one so sensitive,

Still so alert, too, keeping on the shelf
Your Homer and your Cicero
We read together long ago—
You've lost and kept yourself.

You seemed in youth a soul who would arise
To something almost glorious.
You haven't—but Theocritus
Your heart still satisfies.

And so with pipe and book you often sit
In afternoons the window near,
And read, nor note the window's blear,
Nor trucks that trouble it.

How is it life reduced you to this botch
Of night watch at the mattress factory,
With sleep till afternoon to be
Ready again to watch?

And only this brief daylight time that frees
Your thought in any leisure hour
To visualize the watchman's tower,
And chorus of Sophocles.

Or in the stillness of the night, the dark
Ways through the boxes, do you trace
Old scenes, recall a vanished face,
Or hear the meadow lark

We heard together? Do you wonder, too,
What all the years have been about?
How all the flames we knew are out—
All out but I and you!

George, Frank, Will, Chalmer, Ed, are gone.
Yet years they lived and buffeted
The waves, then vanished unbestead
While high noon still was on.

Some rise above a wife, and make her hate
Rungs for ambition; but another slips
Sometimes from knots or broken clips—
Yours is a secret fate,

You never told me, and we meet at times
Only to talk about the long ago
Of Homer and of Cicero,
And say remembered rhymes;

And speak of springs and gardens that we made,
When as a boy you never seemed to plan
What you would be when grown a man;
While I was rapt, afraid

For the years ahead. So I recall your way
There by the onion bed you hoed,
Or by the radish bed I sowed,
Calm as you are to-day.

So I recall your school days, college years
Studious and dutiful and promising.
What worm, what blight, what hidden sting,
What hook, what pruning shears

Wounded you, Edwin, and your life reduced
Clear eyed and minded with no open splotch
Down to your dreary duties as night watch
Still happy, but bemused

Through nights of watching, but with dreams
Amid the city's rattle and lights
Of fields, of Bernadotte, of heights
By which Spoon River streams.

Bernadotte

Spoon River still flows on, even as the years
Have also flown, since that William Walters traded
Some fifty deer skins for this shore, invaded
Later by packing plants, the grist mills' gears.
The wooded hills about this peaceful spot
Bore the white cloud, and looked upon the stream,
And the fishers, pleasure seekers, while in a dream
Like a mirrored image slumbered Bernadotte.

For years lived here that bookman Dr. Strode
Who gathered mussel shells, and studied nature,
And wrote about the flowers, and every feature
Of the landscape, as about the hills he rode.

He sent his specimens of plants and shells
To scientists afar, his observations
To magazines, the learned of other nations;
Meanwhile there was the murmur of the mills'
Wheels by the water turned. Long since he left;
And now the mill in ruin stands, and only
A few deserted houses, looking lonely,
Remembering of what they are bereft.

Near Fourth Bridge

Here in the swamp where the dulled river sweeps
To the Illinois, the sand flats are aglow
With smartweed in the bottoms, there below
The hills on which the oaks are fast asleep.
It is November, but a butterfly
Stumbles along the air, now growing harsh,
And like a man in death the marsh
Lies stiff in silence under a sunset sky.

A hawk sails overhead, braving the sun;
And crows flap flying toward the wood;
Night deepens, and absorbs the solitude,
A zephyr out of nowhere seems to run
Along the waste of cattails, and reveals
An inner meaning, as if the summer's face,
Or some memorial thing sought now this place
Of noisy mallard ducks and blue-winged teals.

Out of the sky they circle to the shore
Of rattling stalks, where the cold willows stand,
The barren willows in a frosted land.
With whirring wings and quacking, with a roar
Of wings they blot the sun, the frozen scum
Around the cattails dims, the sun-set's light
Grows faint, because of their descending flight;
Silence creeps like a wave, for night is come.

Still down they fly like autogyros that wheel
With level planes, and vertically sink
Through dregs of sunset to the silver-steel

Gray of the waters, splotched at last with pink.
Down, down they drop, and make the waters splash
And with rejoicing swim among the reeds;
And now the far-away horizon bleeds,
The sun is gone with one expiring flash.

The hunters have departed. In the East
The planet Jupiter sails like a cresset borne
By magic and no hand. Mists make forlorn
The waters, rising as the exorcist,
The hooded night, convokes them. Behind the hill
The sun has hidden, and the marsh is caught
As by enchantment. Finding what they sought
The ducks are silent, and the marsh is still.

The Sign

There's not a soul on the square,
And the snow blows up like a sail,
Or dizzily drifts like a drunken man
Falling, before the gale.

And when the wind eddies it rifts
The snow that lies in drifts;
And it skims along the walk and sifts
In stairways, doorways all about
The steps of the church in an angry rout.
And one would think that a hungry hound
Was out in the cold for the sound.

But I do not seem to mind
The snow that makes one blind,
Nor the crying voice of the wind—
I hate to hear the creak of the sign
Of Harmon Whitney, attorney at law:
With its rhythmic monotone of awe.
And neither a moan nor yet a whine,
Nor a cry of pain—one can't define
The sound of a creaking sign.

Especially if the sky be bleak,
And no one stirs however you seek,
And every time you hear it creak
You wonder why they leave it stay
When a man is buried and hidden away
Many a day!

The Hills of Big Creek

Hills around Big Creek, and you fields of corn
Whose glistening banners flutter the summer sun,
Behold me once again! After long years
Of wandering in the world, and after cities
East, west, and south explored; and after lives
Laid on my being one by one, like these
Layers of rock which over this little stream
Show the earth's age, each stratum flooring down
And sealing from itself the era gone,
Do I come here once more, and see how earth
Retains its aspect, while the race of men,
Like the new creatures of each passing spring
Are born, grow old, and mix with earth again.
The future to which I looked when as a boy
I gathered flowers here, or these valleys walked,
Or raced these hills, has come, and is the past.
Time like the water flowing through these banks
Takes on the images of fleeting things:
Clouds, sunlight, stars, the spring or winter sun.
That which has flowed will flow. And future days
Were Time as even the days before were Time.
While what was mirrored in the creek was life,
Was grief or happiness, or love or loss,
Which vanished ere the water moving on
Changed the essential mirror.
                              Scarce a face
Of those I knew about these hills remains,
Their beauty to revisit, and recall
With me, if memory served us, what we felt,
Or dreamed, or suffered forty years ago.

All, like the generations of the birds
Which made these woodlands ring about us, even
Their nestlings of the after-years are gone;
While the same song is sung, and while this stream,
As it were the very water that I saw,
Reflects the cloud shaped as it was of old.
Cattle are here, and once again the corn
Rises to make the boundless acres green,
Remembering not the fields which men long dead
Planted and gathered. And here again are youths
And maidens who repeat my happiness,
My wonder at the sailing cloud, my shouts
To comrades hidden in the fastnesses.
They know me not. They know not as a boy
These hills were mine, which now are theirs. O Earth,
Growth is forgetfulness, and within ourselves
Life has its eras, and with senseless stone
Walls in the heart, till to its inner core
Remembrance, like a fallen acorn caught
Between the crevice of great boulders, dies
For light and rain, grows pale and withers too,
Forgetting what it was.
                And those, my chums,
Who my delight companioned, after years
Of world's affairs, of failure, of success,
Of marriage, children, all that we call life,
Have glided to the grave. The future days
To which they lifted eyes, and sang the heart
Of hope and longing, came to them and fled.
Time flowed between their helpless fingers, they
Were but the mocking cloud upon the stream.

If death end all remembrance, what is life
Which blots remembrance of the soul you were
But death? What am I even who only know
This branch called I back to the parent trunk
Of parent days extends, nor can relive
Their feelings, visions, thoughts? This latest twig
Of being, tipped with present life concerned
With this today, lives not the life between.
It has its leaves, which have no memory

Of the many leaves along the branch's growth,
And what they felt of rain and summer sun,
Of cold and frost.   Nor is my being saved
From the death of living to this oblivious tip
By the mind's summoned image of a face,
A girl's, who in obliterate springs with me
Looked on these hills. Nor is that death annulled
By love confessed out of the conscious mind
Which graved what was. To know, the heart must feel;
To remember, it must live again its love.
Hence is this death not overcome by thought
Acknowledging the grief of sundered hands,
And for her death in early youth, these more
Than thirty years gone by. All this I know,
But with the mind, as if an eye should bud
Upon the branch's tip, and backward look
To the parent trunk, but being but an eye,
Without a heart to make the vision life,
Would stare without a tear. And not to feel
Is not to live; it is the loss which life
Exacts for living; it is the death which creeps
With years into the flesh.   She has become
One with these hills, which I but look upon
With an eye for nature still, but deeply changed.
She is to me as if she never was,
Or ever was a part of earth. I see
This landscape in a light that shows each bare,
Each empty spot, each shrunken height, each vale
Made narrow, and these grassy banks reduced
By the cold glare which is Eternity's.
That we forget the soul we were is death;
But that we neither live the past nor grieve,
Proves Death the healer, since he heals in life.

Havana and Lewistown

Havana is now, but more in time will be
A storied spot that treasures up the merry
Days of the Taylor House, the river ferry
Of Ossian Ross and Samuel Mallory;
Days when the steamboats huddled like resting ducks
Below the bordering sand hills, where after hauling
Their seines to shore, to one another calling,
The fishers piled their catches on the trucks.

First there were Indians, and whiskey exchanged for fur,
Then steamboats and their daily sailings,
Loaded from wagons, from the trailings
Through Fulton County, bringing provender,
Hogs, sheep for shipment from the neighborhood
To Chicago and New Orleans, while Havana
Drowsed on the shore, and like an iguana
Increased its flesh and furnished the country food.

The sandy acres near raised richest crops
Of canteloupes and water melons;
The court house gathered felons
From the Spoon River bottoms. The word that lops
Dead limbs and water sprouts was in the square
By Douglas and by Lincoln spoken:
The age fell down, was broken,
But still the river and the town were here.

Still it is here, and still the Taylor House,
The broad streets flanked by bungalows, old dwellings
Of brick, bespeaking the past with wellings

Of memory which the quiet scenes arouse.
Ten miles beyond is Lewistown, just across
The upland rich in legend and in story
Of notables, and all the faded glory
Of Ossian Ross, and his son Lewis Ross.

Gone is the court house, in the long ago
By Newton Walker built; gone houses, churches,
Gone streets, however the looker searches;
Gone Proctor's Grove, gone Spudaway below
The village hills, gone with the populace
That walked about, and vanished like a vapor.
For at last a story printed on fragile paper
Outlasts all bronze, all stone that chisels chase.

Sources of the Poems

Sources of the Poems

Poems are listed below the works of Edgar Lee Masters in which they were originally published. Page citations are to the present anthology.

Along the Illinois. Prairie City, IL: James A. Decker, 1942. Copyright © 1942 by Edgar Lee Masters.

A Book of Verses. Chicago: Way & Williams, 1898.

The Great Valley. New York: Macmillan, 1916; London: Laurie, 1916. Copyright renewed 1944 by Edgar Lee Masters.

The Harmony of Deeper Music: Posthumous Poems of Edgar Lee Masters. Edited by Frank K. Robinson. Austin: Humanities Research Center, Univ. of Texas, 1976. Copyright © 1976 by Ellen Coyne Masters.

Illinois Poems. Prairie City, IL: James A. Decker, 1941. Copyright © 1941 by Edgar Lee Masters.

Invisible Landscapes. New York: Macmillan, 1935. Copyright © 1935 by Edgar Lee Masters.

More People. New York & London: Appleton-Century, 1939. Copyright © 1939 by Edgar Lee Masters.

The Open Sea. New York: Macmillan, 1921. Copyright renewed 1949 by Edgar Lee Masters.

Poems of People. New York & London: Appleton-Century, 1936. Copyright © 1936 by Edgar Lee Masters.

Songs and Satires. New York: Macmillan, 1916; London: Laurie, 1916. Copyright renewed 1944 by Edgar Lee Masters.

Herbert K. Russell is Director for College Relations at John A. Logan College, Carterville, Illinois. A native Illinoisan, he received his Ph.D. degree in English from Southern Illinois University at Carbondale, where he taught the subject and subsequently served as Editorial Writer and Technical Editor at the university's Coal Research Center. He has also edited a new edition of Mary Tracy Earle's Civil War novel *The Flag on the Hilltop*, as well as a collection of photographs taken during the Great Depression, *A Southern Illinois Album: Farm Security Administration Photographs, 1936–1943*—both published in the Southern Illinois University Press' Shawnee Books series. A noted Masters scholar who has written widely on the poet's life and works, Russell has recently contributed an article about the writer to the *Dictionary of Literary Biography*.